rhapsody 2019
an anthology of guelph poetry

Vocamus Press
Guelph, Ontario

Presented by Vocamus Writers Community

Published by Vocamus Press
© All rights reserved

Cover painting of the Petrie Building
by Barbara Salsberg Mathews, 2019
© All rights reserved

ISBN 13: 978-1-77422-003-0 (pbk)
ISBN 13: 978-1-77422-004-7 (ebk)

Vocamus Press
130 Dublin Street, North
Guelph, Ontario, Canada
N1H 4N4

www.vocamus.net

2019

Preface

Rhapsody is an annual collection of poetry by writers in Wellington County, presented by Vocamus Writers Community, a non-profit community organization that supports literary culture in Guelph, Ontario.

The anthology is a celebration of local writing that includes both authors who are well established in their craft and those who are published here for the first time, reflecting the writers and writing that formed the literary communities of Guelph during the year 2018/2019.

The cover art was provided by Barbara Salsberg Mathews. The cover and interior were designed by Jeremy Luke Hill.

Acknowledgments

The Rhapsody Anthology is produced by Vocamus Writers Community, a non-profit community service organization that supports writing, publishing, and book culture in the Guelph area.

This season our work has been generously supported by June Blair, Nick Dinka, Gloria Ferris, Alec Follett, Martina Freitag, Joy Lynn Goddard, Jaya James, Kathleen James, David Muttart, John Nyman, Bob Simmons, Deb Stark, Thanasis Stengos, and Katie Wilde. We appreciate their support very much. If you'd also like to support the work of Vocamus Writers Community you can do so by searching us on www.fundrazr.com.

Thanks to all the contributors for sharing their work so generously. Special thanks to Barbara Salsberg Mathews for allowing her art to be used for the book cover. Thanks finally to all those who contribute to the literary culture of Guelph as readers, writers, publishers, sponsors, venues, broadcasters, and in countless other ways – this collection is a celebration of all that you do.

Table of Contents

Opeongo   1
Paul Hoy

Remembering Shubham   3
Nina Kirkegaard

Spirit   5
Michael Kleiza

Binary   7
Robin Elizabeth Downey

Asphyxia   9
Jeremy Luke Hill

Leaving Siros   11
Bieke Stengos

So This Is How It Feels   13
Donna McCaw

Swan Song   15
Elaine Chang

Agape in Georgian Bay   17
Barb Minett

Night Swim   19
James Clarke

Grandma's House   21
Rob O'Flanagan

penumbra   23
Darcy Hiltz

Her First Poem   25
Valerie Senyk

Life Force   27
Melinda Burns

Flaxseeds   29
Candace De Taeye

Storm   31
Nicholas Ruddock

Flood and time   35
Morvern McNie

Deep Abiding   37
Michelle McMillan

hotel chiaroscuro: a photograph   39
Jeffrey Reid Pettis

torture   41
Adam Maue

Falconry   43
Robert Penfold

The Queen 45
Andy Perry

The Distance 47
Tom Vaine

Dance 49
Sandy Bassie

The St. John's Crowd 51
Sheila Koop

Opeongo
Paul Hoy

Paul Hoy is a poet residing in Guelph, Ontario. His poetry is shaped by the natural landscape and the wilderness of northern Canada. He admires the poetry of Jim Harrison, Jack Gilbert and Seamus Heaney and the prose of Ernest Hemingway, Richard Ford and Cormac McCarthy. He studied English Literature at the University of Toronto.

Opeongo

If I could take back
every word,
now
to settle
back between
us,
our
silence,
our highest
branches,
thinly touching.
No word for 'us' —
only the wild guesswork
of wind, the
tips of our tongues
grasping for the
taste of it, already
tasting the end.
Remember that afternoon
we left together,
coming off
Lake Opeongo
the wind busy

scattering
its big islands of white clouds
crossing the dash
like Thomson's 'Summer Day',
you turning
to peer away,
drawing me in, then,
to the reflection of
you — green and
blue hills
of birch, nearly
transparent,
tamarack,
slender and
teetering.

Remembering Shubham
Nina Kirkegaard

Originally from Quebec City, Nina Kirkegaard is proud to call herself a Guelphite. She is of Bolivian and Danish descent. Nina studied communication, minoring in philosophy and fashion at Ryerson University, and is now studying French at University of Guelph. She writes poetry in English, French, and occasionally Spanish.

Remembering Shubham

Don't diminish him to a news headline
They pleaded, in between the tears

When our friend brought you along
June on MacDonnell

I wide-eyed your liquid purity
It drowned the bar in something better

While our encounters count on one hand
Each gifted me with new energy

Don't diminish him to a news headline
But I need to explain

How treacherous it feels
To know someone for four nights

Dispersed throughout the season
And for him to leave in the winter

Migrant bird, you flew in
Departed with haste

Never to come back
Leaving so many of us distraught

This poem only came to life
Because it traded with you

I could've penned others
Eager to share them

With a poet friend
I never knew was next to me.

Spirit
Michael Kleiza

Originally from Montreal, Michael Kleiza now lives in Guelph. Michael's poems have been published in various anthologies and magazines. His poem "Remembrance Song" was a finalist for the William Collins Canadian Poetry Prize presented by Descant *magazine. He has read at many venues, including The Fringe of the Eden Mills Writers' Festival, the Hillside Festival and the Art Bar in Toronto. He is an alumnus of the Wired Writing program at the Banff Centre for Creativity in Alberta. His firstcollection of poetry,* A Poet on the Moon *(Vocamus Press), was published in 2015.*

Spirit

– For Taylor Mitchell: an old soul in a young body

The two coyotes had picked up her scent and knew her –
knew her for what she was –
knew her as one of their own –
sensed their spirit – sensed their spirit in her
and that it needed to be returned –
put back into the pack.
And so they followed her –
tracked her movements
hidden in the thickets –
hidden in the bushes at the side of the road where she walked.
And when it was time, she knew them –
knew them for what they were –
and she knew herself for what she was.
She removed her scarf – undid it and offered her throat. The blood
released and her spirit – her spirit
came forth and she became them again.

Binary
Robin Elizabeth Downey

Robin Elizabeth Downey was born under a much different name in Toronto, Ontario in 1952. Her collection of erotic stories, Every Way I Know How, *was released in the spring of 2015. She has long been working on a collection of poetry that she feels might be nearing completion. She now makes her home in Guelph, Ontario.*

Binary

    they orbit me,
    two mutually
    eclipsing moons

    engender twice
    the pull of tides
    that surface me

    never suspect
    my two-faced need
    for their twin loves

Asphyxia
Jeremy Luke Hill

Jeremy Luke Hill is the publisher at Gordon Hill Press, a literary publisher based in Guelph, Ontario. He is also the Managing Director at Vocamus Writers Community, a non-profit community organization that supports book culture in Guelph.

Asphyxia

We sign ourselves over
like powers of attorney,
again, though they'll just pull
the plug, leave us un-trached,

to gape our fish-mouths
of wide-eyed heartache,
clutch at bed rails, gasp
out breaths like lost futures –

a death we've died before,
we figure, and who knows,
this time we may survive
the defibrillating jolt.

What's one asphyxiation
more, for old time's sake.

Leaving Siros
Bieke Stengos

Bieke was born in Belgium, came to Canada as a young woman, and has lived here ever since, with time spent in various countries overseas. She has published a chapbook, Aunt Ida, *two collections of poetry,* Abandoned by the Muse *and* Transmigrator.

Leaving Siros

As the ferry leaves
to the playful melody
of its closing gate
it pushes her heart
up to her throat,
while it careens to complete
an artful circle
from the tiny harbour
to the open sea.

When the vessel settles,
it drives deep sorrow
into pockets
that will be emptied later,
when the smells
of coffee and gasoline
bring back the cost
of all she has lost.

So This Is How It Feels
Donna McCaw

Donna McCaw has written five books: Sing a Song of Six Packs, *which claims to remember the 1960's;* Spiral to the Heart *and* The Spell of Crazy Love, *which are both poetry collections;* Under the Apple Boughs, *shorts stories about rural living in Ontario and Saskatchewan; and* It's Your Time, *a nonfiction title about getting ready for retirement.*

So This Is How It Feels

So this is how it feels…
Open heart symphony
Your cheek bone under mine
Breathing slowly together
Your hand on my hip
The other tangled in my hair

Soft curved spaces between us

This is how it feels
You whisper, "I love you."
I whisper back
Enveloped in a sensuous spell
A long mutual sigh
Soft-eyed tears down our cheeks

And we hold each other bone to bone hard

Swan Song
Elaine Chang

Elaine Chang teaches critical theory, literatures and cultures of resistance, and creative writing at the University of Guelph.

Swan Song

In this room the young folk come and go, sure and safely
Sane, relieved to take their leave, this time, say, of
      Baudelaire, his so-called frère, or flowers
      He called evil for some unknown reason.

In these parts the peach part of our growing season's
Short. Like sad sack meals ingested between classes
Wherein I've failed again, or further failed, to help them care
Much at all—about Prufrock's hair, say, much less his despair.

These window-panes, rasped by chain-mail blinds and
Hail-deranged quatrains, halting lines in any kind of
Weather, warn against a world beyond—the wider,
Colder space to which these windows never open.

I've measured out my life in iambs, strong prescriptions
For new glasses, hedging slashes, pencil-parceled bits of
Pippa Passes, Pale Ramons, and dashes—all while what might
Have been an overwhelming question feigns a bow and
Quits this room through stained loose leaves for curtains.

Directions, portents—all uncertain. Diacritical marks, parentheses
Encrypt my former face. I care that I grow old, I grow old, I
Wear rolls above my trousers, hold chalk without conviction.

                                    Still, truth be told—
Indecision dries dissembled in recirculated air. I've heard me disappear
Inside my diction, forgetting my last question, and with it that much more
Of what I once dared to call a calling, if only to myself. A student, then,
Was more like me, or I like her. There was so much more time, then,
For all our visions and revisions. We read fast, then, past "nor" and "neither,"
Placed far bigger bets on "and"—yes, on "and"—and "or," and "either."

Whose murmurs in my ears now impede my leave, (as if) on my own volition?
What could be called my own terms, whatever those would be—were
    I neither not quite me, nor not quite her,
    Neither now mon semblable, nor ma soeur?

Agape in Georgian Bay
Barb Minett

In 1973 Barb Minett happily gave up teaching and began her career as a bookseller. She has been amazed every day since by the ideas and stories that the book world has created. If asked to create a literary dinner party she would certainly invite Charles Darwin, Emily Dickinson, Maggie O'Farrell, Carol Shields, Chris Hedges, and John Le Carre.

Agape in Georgian Bay

That summer
it was a sweet pleasure
to watch
the sun brown your skin
while you lay on the rocks.

A brief respite before you
and your gang hurled
yourselves off the dock-
making up new dives
with mythic names.

Around the World!
The High Fly!
The Cannonball that Drowned the Earth!

Each day
your body became
more confident
shaping any act
coming up laughing.

And I can taste my own adolescent summer.
The joy that came with being released
from everything
but a body in motion.
The feeling of travelling from wet to dry to wet,
from cold to warm to cold,
over and over and over.

I want
to ride a lightning bolt
across the dark of night
see the sky lit
by black and white,
catch a glimpse
of how it fits.

Night Swim
James Clarke

James Clarke was born in Peterborough, Ontario and attended McGill University and Osgoode Hall. He practiced law in Cobourg, Ontario before his appointment to the Bench in 1983. Clarke served as a judge of the Superior Court of Ontario and is now retired, residing in Guelph, Ontario. He is the author of many volumes of poetry and several memoirs.

Night Swim

I dive into the moonless lake – the hills
      a smudge on the far horizon, cut
through the cold dark waters without
      clothes or caution, leaving no stitch
behind, learning how to ride my breath,
      swim freely, palms joining and parting,
joining and parting like a prayer, uncertain
      where I started or where I'm going – no
luminous clear path to follow – yet knowing
      that the lake is sovereign, nourished by
springs too deep for words, trusting
      it will hold me up.

From *Stray Devotions – Prayers, Poems and Intercessions from the Bench* (2018), reprinted with the permission of the author.

Grandma's House
Rob O'Flanagan

Rob O'Flanagan has been a newspaper reporter, photojournalist and columnist for nearly twenty years. He is the author of The Stories We Tell *and* The Blown Kiss Collection, *two volumes of short fiction. He writes, performs and records poetry, and is a visual artist. His collection of poetry,* Open Up the Sky: A Poetic Conversation, *co-authored with Heather Cardin, is available from Vocamus Press.*

Grandma's House

All of this life
makes me want to
return to the tiny room
in grandma's clapboard
house in town.
Christ on the cross
clinging to a cracked
lath and plaster wall.
Pressed copper picture
of quaint Old England.
Small window looking
down on the garden.
Tin soldiers and
cotton bags of pennies
buried here and there
in the yard.
Big breakfasts before
school, lessons in math,
poetry and prayer, games
of rummy and cribbage
before sound sleeps in
the little bed.

penumbra
Darcy Hiltz

Darcy Hiltz is an Archivist / Librarian at Guelph Public Library, where he manages archival records and provides reference services to the public. In his spare time he writes poetry, is an avid student, tends to his family's history, swims, and assists his father on his farm during the summer and fall. He is married and lives in Fergus.

penumbra

my shadow
e
l
o
n
g
a
t
e
d
on snow

the sun
casts
judgement
inflates
mocks
like
a carnival mirror
twisting the darkness
inside

Her First Poem
Valerie Senyk

Valerie Senyk is a multi-media artist. She received her BFA and MA in Drama from the University of Saskatchewan, and taught university Theatre Arts for over 23 years. She is a playwright, an actor, and a published and recorded performance poet. She has published a full-length volume of poetry, I Want A Poem *(Vocamus Press, 2014).*

Her First Poem

a July dawn gleams clean
and bright with God

she pedals still and empty streets
strange joy dancing in her ribcage

abandons her maroon bicycle
in a park too early for the playground crowd

pulls from her pocket
a folded paper with her first poem

divines, as only the young can,
the voice that she will use to speak

a pen breaking open
her future

Life Force
Melinda Burns

Melinda Burns is a writer and a psychotherapist in private practice in Guelph, Ontario, where she also teaches writing. Her writing has won awards for fiction, including first prize in the Toronto Star Short Story contest in 2001 and first prize in the Elora Writers' Festival Writing Contest in 2008. She has published poems in various magazines, read her essays on CBC radio, and published essays on writing in Canadian Notes and Queries *and in K.D. Miller's book on creativity and spirituality,* Holy Writ.

Life Force

My neighbour called me an Angel of Mercy
for drowning the injured mouse, I found on my lawn
but she didn't see it struggle for life
throw out its little legs in its effort to live
as I held it under the water
in the stone bird bath.

How adamant it was for life.

I've heard people tell me
about wanting to die,
anguish in their eyes
I try to keep them afloat
with words

impart the life force that even
the smallest dying creature has.

Flaxseeds
Candace De Taeye

Candace de Taeye's poetry has been published in CV2, Carousel, Echolocation, Feathertale.com *and* Joypuke. *Her first chapbook,* Roe, *was published by PS Guelph in 2015. Her debut full-length collection,* Small Planes and the Dead Fathers of Lovers, *was published by Vocamus Press in 2016.*

Flaxseeds

Pinhead, flax or apple seed and hypodermic knife penis. Isabella Rossellini shouts 'Seduce Me!' in spandex but everyone else is ashamed. Hiding their linens. Coats wrapped tight vestigial wing nubs. Rape-y bastards, traumatically inseminating each other right in the gut. You need to steam them as if trying to get a good froth from skim milk. Kafka into book spine. Diatomaceous earth arcs apartment doors. Optimistic protection, like garlic for other sexier hematophages. Females rarely emit their alarm pheromone, unlike the topped gluttonous misread males. Sultry harborage smells of rotten raspberries. Rostrum into your nape, thighs, even that little pocket behind your knee. Studies hypothesize resisting may be higher than the cost of consent. Bean leaves Balkan magic Velcro. Thank DDT for fifty years without that phantom itch. Bed, bath and beyond the bald eagle omelets.

Storm
Nicholas Ruddock

Nicholas Ruddock is author of The Parabolist *(Doubleday 2010),* How Loveta Got Her Baby *(Breakwater 2014), and* Night Ambulance *(Breakwater 2016).*

Storm

Hurricane off Cuba
coiled, spinning counter-clockwise,
muscling up the coast
juiced on anabolic steroids,
on drugs spilled from the bodies
of weightlifters, athletes,
others prone to excess,
on by-products of this illegality and that,
on ritalin, cocaine, methamphetamine,
oxycontin, percocet, fentanyl,
party-time hydrocarbons,
date-rape chemicals swirling down
toilets and shower drains,
percolating through groundwater,
spouting into towering clouds of microbes
catalyzed by seawater too hot, too hot,
the Gulf Stream shying away
from Florida, from the Carolinas,
from estrogens, contraceptives,
testosterone, no-cal sweeteners,
breath freshener, caffeine,
bodywash, SPF 30,
lead, mercury, hexavalent chromium,
plastic bags blistered on chainlink,
iceberged chunks of styrofoam,
acid oozing from batteries

lime-green and fluorescent,
9 volts on the skin
of alligators, muskrats, watersnakes,
rain drumming down
on container loads of contraband,
guys with acne scrambling for higher ground,
faces on TV saying "shipwreck,"
"mountainous waves,"
multinational sailors on flags of convenience,
ballasts shifting,
teenage migrants
tiptoeing like acrobats,
tankers tipped, pallets busted,
splinters of steel, wood, composite,
stormwater bubbling up through sewers,
E. coli, typhoid, windows ex- and im-
ploded, food banks shuttered,
mothers pushed down in beds and alleyways,
children standing in cribs,
tenements, condos, ruptured kitchens,
downtown hospital supply rooms vandalized,
saline, surf, surge, sandbar,
shorebirds battened down,
spartina flattened in Chesapeake Bay,
lobsters holding tight, bug-eyed,
Hudson River porpoises moving out
to Gaspé, Baie-des-Chaleur, Port aux Basques,
this tropical storm coiling
out of Cuba of all places,
Castro, Guevara, Communism,
the thin and hungry ones,
fruit rotting on the ground,

rafts on the beaches,
Russians, the Bay of Pigs,
AK-47s strewn through bracken,
detritus of corporate welfare,
hedge funds, looters, computers,
Putin, Blair, the Clintons,
anti-vaxxers,
and we should have known about this
last week, last month, last year,
before we put the babies to bed,
before the lights were turned out,
the recoil,
we should have seen it coming,
felt the kickback in the mangroves,
Katrina, New Orleans,
anywhere south of Miami,
voodoos in Port-au-Prince
suspecting it all along,
eyes as quiet as Zen,
fingers palsied,
hell to pay,
water rising,
fury fed by everything
we did and didn't do,
isobars twitching on the maps
we drew in high school,
the Aztec, the Maya,
the Spanish swallowing molten gold,
murderers, murderers,
the dodo, the auk,
shark-fin soup in restaurants,
elephants sun-bloated for their tusks,

conceit, control, primacy,
the India-rubber ball
thrown hard against the wall,
No, we didn't ask for this, not
directly,
aquifers of poison being
sucked skyward
but here we are,
the weather made for us and
by us,
courtesy of Newton's Third
Law, 1787,
two hundred and thirty years
of pushing, pushing, pushing,
and finally this,
this screaming,
this wind.

Flood and time
Morvern McNie

Morvern McNie writes poetry and short fiction. She lived in Guelph for over twenty years and is now living in Elora. She has performed at Hillside Festival and the Eden Mills Fringe. Her work appears on two Guelph compilation CD's called Work Songs *and* 60 Second Songs, *both produced by Lewis Meville. She is currently working towards publishing a chapbook of poems and short fiction.*

Flood and time

After the flood they are there
on the hill outside my window.
They stand holding hands in the sun.
Scattered in the grass are things:
a silver bowl, loose plastic sheets with photos,
a legless doll, a gold trophy,
a blue sequined dress, a painted guitar.
They protect them from an unbearable loss.
I want to give them all a home.
Each a room where they can place their things.
Where they can sit at the table and eat a good meal.
Where they can tell me the story of who they are,
where they've been, how they'll live.
I want to let them know I am stuck behind this window.
I can see through it but it moves with my steps.
Always this window – separating me.
My eyes begin to water, a blur of souls.
I hear the painted guitar
its tints and shades, flood and time
drawing me near beyond the glass pane.

Deep Abiding
Michelle McMillan

Michelle McMillan is a Horticultural Therapist and Therapeutic Touch Practitioner. From 2003 to 2012 she designed, edited and published TongRen, *the journal of the Canadian Taiijquan Federation. She has written a collection of poems and memoirs and has studied writing with Melinda Burns, Lorraine Gane, and Brian Henry.*

Deep Abiding

Clouds gather in the prairie sky,
break the sere infinity of solitude.
Any dalliance is welcome

where sunsets are too wide for lonely eyes,
and a glance that lingers too long on the lips
causes unbearable thirst.
Those clouds will burst and it will rain
but the relief will be fleeting.
A flush of affection never satisfies
the impoverished land.

These sediments of ancient waters
were deposited here too long ago
to recall depths of cool blue light.

I am old now, well worn.
In this displaced sea,
under a hot red sky,
I buried a husband too young to forget
and a child too young to remember
our poor past,
the damp wild green of our homeland.

Vestiges of passing texture this landscape: ruts
left by those who rolled over and moved on, pits
from the strain of weight-bearing hooves, holes
that break a horse's leg in seconds, the echo
of one merciful bullet through the brain, traces
of scavengers scuffed by carcass drag.

All comes to dust and blows away,
settles into compromise,
like the caked foundation on the faces of public women;
those bold, undemanding rudbeckia
who live on dust
and whatever they are given.
Enough to set seed.

Here fresh withers and dies,
cold brittles all to silver,
blends with wolf willow, piles of bones,
the highlights in once-dark hair.

But the roots survive in deep abiding.

hotel chiaroscuro: a photograph
Jeffrey Reid Pettis

Jeffrey Reid Pettis lives and works in Guelph as an educator. He listens to loud music loudly and his academic interest in literary depictions of paranoia is a fine line of yarn away from a conspiracy theory wall. He mostly sits around and reads, sometimes writes poems, and even more sometimes publishes them.

hotel chiaroscuro: a photograph

with the curtains not quite closed,
an intruding strip of blue sunrise
(or so it appears in the photograph)
forces the hands of the clock open,
makes it tether time back to itself.
no more citrus-and-shadow mystery
hours. no bubble baths and chopin.
no, now is the hour of stolen night-
stand bibles, alphabetized by sin,
of white towels pooled on roasted
hardwood floors or black hole shag,
of returning everything to its proper
place. the light that took its shelter
in the corners of the room at night
now ascends the couch and creeps up
wood slat walls in artificial sunrise.
the lampshade halo fades from gold
to beige and hangs askew. the room
orbits the floor lamp and its broken
switch, the last bastion against in-
betweens. check-out is at eleven; late
guests are subject to additional charges.

torture
Adam Maue

Adam Maue moved to Guelph on a whim in 2016. Since then he's worked odd jobs, volunteered, and made friends there during the winter, and he's spent his summers traveling Canada by train. He hopes to keep doing what he's doing until the next adventure comes along.

torture

i asked the telephone company to unplug me,
the lock fitters to double the bolts,
the birds to stop singing.
there was a morning flower blooming,
that i needed to cut.
the work was bleeding my body,
my spine was raw.
exhausted,
i hung up my crucifix,
followed the easy path:
i ate pancakes and watched a movie;
it was only slight torture.

Falconry
Robert Penfold

Robert Penfold Bob taught high school English, covering all levels and grades, from 1966 to 2003, in Windsor, Thunder Bay and Haliburton in Ontario, as well as Tarsus, Turkey. Bob is an occasional composer of short verse and short fiction, and a charter member of the Dead Poets Society at the Dominion Hotel in Minden, Ontario.

Falconry

    Despite
      Time and patience
        Invested in this weapon
      Upon first release
    I find myself
hoping
    The hawk
      Will never return
        For whatever comes back
      Will be nothing
    Like a bird

The Queen
Andy Perry

Andy Perry is an avid reader, a poet, and a fiction and non-fiction writer. She served nine years as an Intelligence Officer with the Canadian Army and holds a BA in English Literature from the Royal Military College of Canada and an MFA in Creative Writing from the University of Guelph.

The Queen

She removed her crown
melted it down
made a ring
for every finger in the kingdom

Knocked her castle to the ground
raised a city with the stones
a home for every tired body
tossed by the great storm

She walked the streets in plain clothes
ate plain food, smiled
at every face she passed
young or old, known or unknown

Dismantled her ancient oaken throne –
cracked it to pieces –
kindled a colossal fire
at the center of the city

The blaze reached the sky
breached the long night
blew warmth into every open window
drew the people, one by one
to gather 'round the light

The Distance
Tom Vaine

Tom Vaine lives in Elora, Ontario, and works as a high school teacher in the area. He has a graduate degree in Literature Studies, with a focus on speculative fiction, and spends his reading and writing time working in this genre.

The Distance

This always starts the same way,

Every time I begin
I reshape myself,
pull parts from the muck
I've sunk in on my path
to you.

But the bog between us
is treacherous, I flail
as I step,
stifled and stuck,
some swampthing
lost in the mist.

If you saw me
would you reach me?
Pick the person from
the shambling debris?

Dance
Sandy Bassie

Sandy Bassie has maintained a love of language and a passion for writing her entire life. She reveals this in her journals, reflections on life, poetry, and some (very) short stories. Sandy believes creativity comes in many forms.

Dance

When I was a little girl
Lithe and loose of limb, I danced
Upon the cartage way innocent
To sin, before the world turned me
Round, took childhood away
The dance was mine
And freely flowed
Along the cobbled way
Then came responsibility
Like spokes pushed through my soul
Its burdens anchored hard to me
I could not let them go
Unhobble me
Don't break me
Remind these feet
To play, to
Move with grace
And dignity
Dance through
Every day
Sorrow don't you
Weigh me down
Choke
This tender frame

While grace
Remains
I need to dance
Along the
Cobbled way

The St. John's Crowd
Sheila Koop

Sheila Koop writes poetry, short stories, bits of creative nonfiction and is currently working on a novel for preteens. Her poem "Purple Voyage" won first prize at the 2003 Elora Writer's Festival Competition, and her short story, "The Arcana of Living Springs", was awarded Honourable Mention for the 2014 Elora Writers Festival competition.

The St. John's Crowd

I miss the screech of the seagulls
who careen like sails on air –
my flotilla of hope

squawk and call, circle and gather
their rite of place as they
jostle for the perch with the best view
for stealing.
This is your turf –
where the gull shades,
white and grey and black are
watercolours splashed on salty blue sky.

You loved this view –
oily trawlers of red and yellow
that float in the harbour,
dwarfed by massive naval ships
they groan as they sidle up to the pier.

The bright painted clapboard houses where
you lived and collected rent,
the gull-like opportunist in you.
People nests, lined up the hills like kids

waiting for the bell to ring. Above
the ocean, their blue-green gaze
fixed on freighters and fishing boats
who pass like friends in the Narrows.

You were proud of the climb up Signal Hill –
follow its rise, survey the Atlantic
a perfect sea bird's view
breathe the salt
feel swallowed up: hikers tiny beside
rock fissures where
the ocean roars and hisses.

Our last summer visit with the garrulous gulls –
their shrill language
their restlessness
their constancy.

The faraway life you had with the St. John's crowd;
their laughter poised to tickle the underside of life,
comfortable in their rugged rooms.

The noisy gulls, they make me wonder how to miss you now.

Vocamus Writers Community

Vocamus Writers Community is a non-profit community organization that supports book culture in Guelph and the surrounding area. It runs workshops, writing groups, and writer hang-outs. It offers resources for writers looking to publish their work both traditionally and independently. It promotes readings, launches, and other literary events in the community. It also produces the annual *Rhapsody* anthology Guelph area poetry. For more information, email vocamuswriterscommunity@gmail.com.

www.ingramcontent.com/pod-product-compliance
Lightning Source LLC
Chambersburg PA
CBHW032217040426
42449CB00005B/635